# RICK STEVES

The Biography of Rick Steves

## University Press

# CONTENTS

# INTRODUCTION

**M**any people would jump at the chance to travel for work. For Rick Steves, his entire profession is not only traveling all over Europe, but he gets to immerse himself in popular travel locations. The twist in his work is that he tells his viewers and readers how they can travel in a way that gives them a much more local experience. Since it is easy to get information on the popular aspects of these locations with tourists, he focuses on what the locals enjoy. From important locations and monuments that aren't very well known to great places to eat that are largely known only to locals, Steves gives would-be travelers a wealth of ideas about places where they aren't likely to run into a bunch of other tourists. Of course, some people love to visit all the tourist highlights, but even they like escaping from the crowds and expensive sites. Thanks to Steves, and everyone traveling to nations where he's been, there is a way of finding those activities and events that probably aren't easily found during initial research of a vacation spot.

He has been particularly interested in finding the lesser-known to little-known aspects of different tourist destinations. When he was 14, he started traveling with his parents to look at important locations for those who loved pianos. That included Steves and his family because they ran a piano store in Washington state. For his first trip to Europe, he was already focused on the less frequently visited destinations, giving him a much different experience compared to those who traveled with a focus on tourism. His family focused on pianos, so they were interested in something other than the kinds of places that most people wanted to visit while in Europe. Before he reached adulthood, he had not only traveled to Europe but also learned that there was much more to see and do than most people know about Europe.

With an interesting foundation and idea about what travel should be like, Steves navigated through his teenage years and young adulthood with a different outlook on life. That was when his career path took an interesting turn from the norm- he became a travel writer. Over the next few decades, he started his own business, sharing the secrets of a different kind of traveler. After writing several guidebooks, he gained attention as someone who knew how to make the most of a trip. His writing style and advice earned him a TV and radio show, helping him reach a much larger audience. He also wrote a travel column and started his own website to ensure people had access to his tips and tricks for making the most of vacations, business trips, and travel. He even has his own tourist program that helps roughly 30,000 people experience the lesser-known attractions and a more authentic experience when visiting Europe.

His travels have also given him a look into how people are treated in North America and Europe. As a result, he has become both a political and civic activist. This has led to him being a much more outspoken advocate, which has gotten him some backlash. As an outspoken Climate Change activist, he has tried to incorporate various ways to be more climate-friendly in solutions for travelers. This includes making regular contributions to nonprofit organizations focused on finding solutions to the problems created by climate change. This is similar to the company imposing its own carbon tax to ensure that the tours and other carbon-emitting aspects of the business are offset as much as possible. He is also a supporter of public broadcasting, in large part because that was where he found his footing with his career.

Steves spends about a quarter of the year in Europe conducting his research to ensure that his business continues providing the best advice. This ensures that his ability to help people find the best places to visit and things to do remains current. With such a dedication to his profession, Steves will likely continue to bring travelers who want a unique perspective, advice, and tricks that will help them better understand the locations they visit.

# CHAPTER 1

## *Early Life*

L ong before he was born, the roots for what the well-known traveler would be were planted. His father, Richard John Steves, was adopted after his mother married for a second time. He grew up loving boats and taking on jobs that supported his interest in traveling on the water. Growing up around the Seattle area, the elder Steves had plenty of different bodies of water to explore and enjoy his love of boating.

While his hobby was boating, the elder Steves loved music and sought to turn that love into a career. He attended the University of Washington, earning a musical degree that he then used to start a career as a music teacher, focusing on teaching high school students. In addition to working as a music teacher, he created a second job for himself - working with pianos. Over time he went from being a technician to being a highly respected importer of pianos from Germany. Germany is still known for being among the leading producers of some of the world's best Western musical instruments, including violins and pianos. Over time, this love developed into the retail store *Steves Sound of Music*.

Not long after graduating college, he married June Erna Fremmerlid. She was a first-generation American, with her parents having moved to the country from Norway. The couple had three children: two daughters and a son. They both played important roles in forming their children's opinions and outlooks toward the world around them.

Richard John Steves, Jr. was their first child, and he was born while they were in Barstow, California, on May 10, 1955. They returned to the Seattle area in 1967. They initially set up their family in Kenmore, Washington, but they finally set down roots in Edmonds. This is where Steves, Sr. began working for several high schools and opened his piano business. With a father who loved traveling by boat and a mother who loved visiting Norway, the three kids grew up loving traveling and seeing places not normally seen or visited by tourists. As a homemaker, Juna instilled a love for Western Europe and an idea of what life was like as a native instead of only what was known about traveling from a tourist's perspective. They also attended the local Lutheran Church, a religion that Steves, Jr. has continued to practice over his adult life.

At 14 years old, his parents finally took the family over to Europe, not just to visit the locations where his grandparents had lived but to tour the different piano manufacturing factories. This left a huge impact on the way he viewed traveling. While most people who went to Europe visited popular sites, such as the Black Forest, the Eiffel Tower, Big Ben, and European castles, the Steves family were checking out sites and things that even the locals didn't know about. His first time traveling a long way from home was a vastly different experience for the teenage Steves. He seemed well aware of just how different the experience was. As they traveled around Germany, he kept a record of the trips by writing down details of his travels on postcards. These weren't meant for anyone but his future self, and they remain in his possession as a reminder of how he felt and how that inspired a life of traveling. They took some time to visit his mother's family in Norway, giving the American family a better look at what life was like in that country. There was nothing typical about his first trip to Europe or the experiences that the family had. While that first trip was memorable, no matter how typically touristy it was, it did help him to realize the tone of how people viewed traveling and learning about the places they go to. Instead of treating these locations like places that were just there for visitors, he learned about the locals and the things that were important to them. This outlook ensured that he was just as concerned with the people who lived in these places as he was with what he could get out of being there.

Ironically, their time in Europe occurred during an important point in American history (arguably an important point in world history). Like many people around the world, the Steves family tuned in to watch as the first astronauts landed on the moon and took those first steps. While it was important, and Americans are well aware of how the nation reacted to the achievements sought for an entire decade, Steves saw how the rest of the world viewed this notable event. It is easy to consider it an American accomplishment, but as the astronaut Neil Armstrong said at the time, "That's one small step for man, one giant leap for mankind." Steves saw how this event changed how people in other nations experienced the major event. With this unique perspective, he began observing other aspects of the world abroad. When they went to parks, he started to observe how the people interacted with each other. This was when he started drawing parallels with what he had experienced back home. What stood out to him was how the parents and children interacted. Perhaps because he was still so young, this was the type of relationship that he took note of. He began to think about how parents and children love each other the same way no matter where they live. This made it clear to him that there was a lot about the human experience that was nearly universal. It was a revelation that helped to influence many of his ideas about the world over the rest of his life, particularly his outlook on civic duties and civil rights.

He finished high school in 1973, but his attention was focused on something other than higher education. He was more interested in traveling. Now a young adult, he decided to go out and experience Europe without his family. This became a regular occurrence over the course of his life, traveling both with people and on his own. Each time he left the US to see more sites in Europe, he expanded his ideas about the world and the people who lived in it.

# CHAPTER 2

## *Crash Course*

**W**hen he returned to the US after his first solo visit, Steves did go on to earn a degree. Like his father, he opted to go to the local school, the University of Washington. It remains a university known for providing students with a great education, especially for students with a different outlook on life. With an interest in travel, he seemed to be looking for a career that would allow him to keep visiting Europe and learning about new places and cultures. His first trip to Europe without his family had given him one particularly unique outlook that had not been a concern when he was 14 years old – he had to learn how to manage his own money and budget. This is something that young adults struggle with because this is usually the first time they have to rely on their own financial skills to deal with all of their bills and activities. Many young adults do have help during their initial years, especially when they go to college. Their parents help with expenses like room and board to ensure their children can focus more on their education and learning to be adults. For Steves, he had a crash course in managing a budget because he was traveling on his own. Everything he did and bought had to be funded from his own pocket. During the 1970s, people relied on cash when traveling, especially when they were young. There weren't any debit cards or mobile devices to quickly get money. Because he had to budget to ensure he could enjoy the full trip, Steves learned from a very young age to monitor his expenses and look for ways to save money without losing out on experiences.

Just like he had done at 14 years old, as a young adult, Steves continued to record his travels. Instead of small postcards, the traveler used journals to record more detail and information as he moved around Europe. As he learned how to budget, he made sure to make entries so that he could continue to use the financial tricks going forward. Over the years, the number of journals he had grew exponentially, long after he finished college.

While attending the University of Washington, Steves started sharing his traveling knowledge. Since he lived on North America's west coast, many people around him were more likely to have traveled to Hawaii and Alaska rather than to Europe, which was a much more expensive endeavor. They didn't need a passport to go to the exotic American states, making a trip to Europe seem far too expensive - a pipe dream. But they also had some closer, cheaper options that meant they could enjoy their vacations. Steves was the one who helped to change their minds while he was still a college student. With a growing number of interested students, he started a travel class. The university had a program called The Experimental College that educated students on a range of different topics. Steves was able to start sharing what he had already learned as a part of this program. All classes offered as a part of the program were taken at the student's leisure, so there was nothing to compel students to keep going as they would not get any credits for attending or completing the courses. It also meant that the classes offered were the kinds of things that students wanted to learn about or were seeking to learn more about to see if they were interested in a particular field without having to pay a large amount of money first. Steves knew how to target the types of students interested in learning what he knew about traveling in Europe, naming his class "Travel Europe: Cheap!" This name attracted the attention of people who wanted to go to Europe but were likely to think that it wasn't an option because of how expensive it was. His course's title immediately let people interested in going to another continent know they could do it for much less money than they thought.

Unsurprisingly, this course proved to be incredibly popular. The first interested students who took the course probably shared just how much they had learned with others, eventually making it an absolute "must-take" course for young people interested in traveling. It also gave him an idea about how to travel without going alone while still in college. Like many other students, he did need to work while in school, so he had a job that gave him the means to continue his education – both in college and traveling in Europe. Like his father, Steves loved pianos, so he was a good player in his own right. It also gave him a unique skill that other people wanted to learn, so he was able to start working as a teacher. This was not only a way to make time for playing the piano more regularly, but it helped to hone his teaching skills. This helped him to learn how to better speak to people on topics that were entirely unfamiliar to them. Learning to play the piano is not easy because it requires using both hands equally and a foot on the pedals. A lot about playing the piano is foreign to a student, similar to how budgeting and traveling on a different continent is foreign to other college students. This was one job in which he did what he loved to earn money to support his other job that he did to help others. From there, he decided he could help people tour Europe, resulting in organizing a trip with other students. They rented a minibus and went around the continent, exercising what they had learned in his class.

By the time he was ready for graduation in 1978, Steves already had experience in the field that had his attention – teaching people to travel wisely. He had a dual degree when he walked across the stage, one in business administration and another in European history. The knowledge in both of these areas was used over the coming decades, but neither was nearly as helpful as the experience he gained from teaching a course and taking a group on tour in Europe. Whether or not he knew it, Steves was already well on his way down the unique career path that gained him the attention of PBS. Before he got his own show, though, Steves still had to learn about reaching a wider audience than people of his own age and financial situation.

# CHAPTER 3

## *Traveling on the Cheap*

F ollowing graduation, he continued doing the things that he had done while he was in college. He worked as a piano teacher and continued his course at the university. During summers, he took people over to Europe to help them experience Europe in a way that was far less common at the time – they got to see more of what it was like to live in the places they visited. This different perspective meant they had many more interesting stories because they had seen the sites most people missed by focusing on the tourist sites. Steves had already demonstrated a knack for showing others how to travel on a small budget, targeting a group of people who are notoriously low on cash – college students. They proved to be a great testing ground for his abilities to instruct and refine how he presented information. Teaching people just striking out on their own to budget is very complicated, so what he did went beyond simply helping other college students look for deals – he helped them learn how to budget.

Going forward, Steves no longer needed to provide the same level of teaching because he wanted to reach other adults who were traveling. It wasn't just students who felt that traveling to Europe was little more than a pipe dream – adults with children to those who were retired were interested in going abroad. Still, many felt that visiting European countries would require too much money. Having gone with his family when he was 14, he had a good incentive to want other parents to take their children abroad to better educate them.

No longer in college, he wasn't in a position where he could hold classes to teach people what he knew. Even if he could offer a class, that would only educate people in the local area because the Internet was still a couple of decades from being common in people's homes (in the late 1970s, there were only the early stages of the Internet in existence, but it was still mainly a tool of the military used only within a small network of government agencies). In 1979, the best way to reach a wider audience was to write a book and find a publisher. Traveling abroad wasn't flooded with easily available advice and ideas, so he entered a field with much potential and little competition. He had the added benefit of proven experience in helping others to accomplish the goal of traveling through Europe on a small budget. This gave him credibility and a feel for what information people needed to know to succeed. He had a good idea of what people were interested in seeing and the kinds of areas and attractions they might find interesting. Even in the 1970s, visiting the usual tourist places, like the Eiffel Tower, was more expensive. It meant dedicating a large chunk of the vacation to visiting sites that took only a few hours of a single day. For those interested in getting more from a trip, Steves was able to offer a wealth of other activities that could be carried out over a longer period of time for less than the cost of those one-time tourist traps. This gave readers an idea of what they could do and for how much money as alternatives to the activities that they already knew about—just like with the class he offered, the book that Steves wrote made it clear exactly what to expect from reading the book – *Europe Through the Back Door*. This referred to how people could go into venues or restaurants, gaining great access to things that others enjoyed but at a much lower cost.

Writing a nonfiction book requires tons of research, experience, or both. During a time when research required more time than today, Steves was fortunate because he had already documented everything he needed. He drew from his own experience, which included his personal trials and errors. He had done his research and written it up in a way that was easy to digest. Instead of starting from scratch with his book, Steves took the notes and lecture material he had written while running his classes and started his book. This was a great starting point, but it wasn't enough to complete a full book for a wider audience. To supplement the lecture notes, he had a wealth of information recorded in his journals, things that he had done that were based more on his own interests and experiences. Since he had developed an interest in traveling while he was still with his family, his journals included more details for families than many of his classes had incorporated.

Unfortunately, finding a publisher for the book wasn't particularly easy. The market didn't appear reliable to publishers he approached, probably because there wasn't much competition. This was taken to mean there wasn't much interest, which wasn't true. Like the students at his university, many Americans assumed that they couldn't afford to go to Europe. The book Steves wanted to publish was meant to help dispel that assumption. Unable to find a publisher, he decided to self-publish the book the next year. Self-publishing wasn't quite like it is today, and he still had to go through a publisher. He was able to have 2,500 copies of his book printed a year after he had written it, and it was done through the Snohomish Publishing Company.

At that time, he was still working as a piano teacher. Once his books were printed, he stored all of them in his piano studio. Since they were self-published, it took a lot of work for him to get the books on bookstore shelves, resulting in boxes of books taking up space that he used for his students. They sat on the boxes when they performed in recitals. It did draw attention to his book, though, so people who attended his lessons and the recitals he held were aware of what they were using as seats. Even if he didn't mean to do it this way, it was one way to get the word out about his book without spending money on marketing.

Like the class he had taught, Steves wasn't particularly interested in profiting from the books. They were more of a way of sharing his knowledge with anyone interested in traveling. This was stated at the beginning of the guide: "Anyone caught reprinting any material herein for any purpose whatsoever will be thanked profusely." This starkly contrasts the warnings that any duplication without consent or approval will be prosecuted. Steves wanted his knowledge to be shared so that more people could see what Europe had to offer. He was more than happy to have his knowledge shared, even though it would be a financial loss to himself. Perhaps this was part of what drew more attention to his work. People saw his enthusiasm from the beginning.

# CHAPTER 4

## *An Unintended Career*

**W**ord of mouth proved incredibly powerful as people began to read his book. Whether or not he had intended it, Steves began to gain a reputation for being someone who could help people not only make it to Europe but to have a great time while they were there. When people read his guide, they began to plan their trips. They soon found that his advice was exactly what he had promised – a way of moving around different parts of Europe within a tight budget. It became obvious that such a vacation did not require spending thousands of dollars. The key was treating the trip like you were a native of the area. The expensive touristy stuff cost so much, but by eating at places that the locals loved and doing the kinds of activities that were free across much of Europe, you could afford to travel there. Most nations in Western Europe have a lot of free or low-cost activities. There were plenty of free resources for those interested in learning about the different locations.

What is notable about the first guide he published was that it was not very professional looking. Since he had published it himself, the pages were clearly typed (personal computers were not a common aspect of home life in the early 1980s, and laptops were still about a decade from being developed). The mistakes were erased with liquid whiteout. It made for an incredibly unrefined book. Despite this, the book ended up selling out because of how well people who read it spoke of it. This is impressive on many levels, but it demonstrates his information's value. And how correct he was about people just needing a little more information to finally make that leap to start traveling across the Atlantic. The demand was there, and he didn't have to do much marketing to get the word out.

With no more books left in stock and so much time passing since its publication, he decided to write a second edition. This time, Steves strived to make a book that looked more professional. Instead of typing it up on a rented typewriter, he hired a typesetter to ensure the pages looked the same and didn't show the signs of corrections that were obvious in the first version of his book.

As he worked on an update to the book, he also started a tourism company in the same studio where he taught piano. From there, he started growing a tourist business that used what he had learned in business administration. It also gave him dedicated time to travel, which meant he never had to go without doing one of the things he loved most. Using what he had learned from teaching students in a course, he offered seminars that helped older adults plan for more in-depth trips than college students wanted to see and experience. There was a lot of crossover, but families and senior adults have more to consider than someone traveling as a college student. This meant adjusting the details he included in the sessions, which then translated into some of the information that he added to the new version of the book.

Over time, his classes became so popular that he no longer had time to teach. The music studio became a travel business that used the name of his first book – *Europe Through the Back Door*. Eventually, this was shortened to ETBD because it was easier to remember and say. With piano lessons no longer taking up his time, Steves was able to provide more organization and tours to those who were interested in traveling. Despite the shift in focus, his business remained next to his parents' piano business. Eventually, he moved across the street, but he was also working on his personal life at that time. He married his girlfriend, Anne, and the couple had two children. The marriage did not last, though, and the couple divorced in 2010.

Apart from some basic information, he was able to keep his personal life private, something that likely got more difficult over the next few years as he had caught the attention of people who saw the potential for him to bring his knowledge to a much wider audience than he could with a book.

# CHAPTER 5

## *From Print to TV*

**W**hen he first started advising on traveling, it's unlikely that Steves thought it would become a full-time job. Once it was clear that he could make a pretty good living, he probably felt that he had reached the peak of what he could accomplish. And he was very happy helping those who read his books or had time for his lectures. The fact that he would get to travel as a part of work was a bonus that wanderers all envy when it isn't a part of their jobs.

His success was largely because of his passion for travel, and his desire to make it more accessible to everyone came through in his books. He soon republished the book regularly, and they continued to sell quickly. It demonstrated how well Steves knew his potential audience – just because there doesn't seem to be a demand doesn't mean there isn't one. Over the 1980s, his books grew in popularity until someone decided he was the ideal speaker for European travels, offering him a much bigger platform.

Where most tourist businesses booked the trips and activities, Steves provided a different approach to touring. He didn't book tickets and activities, leaving the activities up to the members of his group to manage their budgets. With such a singular approach, his methods of traveling seemed much more accessible and free-spirited than more traditional travel agencies. His passion and outlook on travel captured the attention of people at the Public Broadcast System, better known as PBS. For decades, this station has put together programming that would interest and inform a large percentage of the public. As it was evident, many Americans were interested in learning more about traveling to Europe, especially if they could get advice on doing it without spending a fortune. This made Steves seem like a near-perfect spokesman and guide, so he was offered to have his own show on their channel.

This would likely be a dream come true. He had grown up in the Pacific Northwest in a family that focused on music. Nearly as soon as he graduated high school, he started figuring out how to travel without relying on someone else to fund his galivanting around new areas. He was able to make his own schedules when he went to Europe, explored areas that weren't covered by the usual guides and tourist agendas, and chatted with the locals to learn more about the cultures (not just their tourist attractions). These were the kinds of things that people wanted to know and how they wanted to experience Europe. Suddenly, the idea that people could go to Europe instead of thinking of it as completely unattainable was becoming more popular among Americans. This is largely thanks to the airing of *Travels in Europe with Rick Steves*, which debuted on PBS in April 1991.

Once again, Steves' approach, energy, and advice proved incredibly popular nationwide. Over the years, people tuned in to get more ideas. Since he was allowed to use the show to promote his own business and books, his business boomed. Given the nature of his books, it made sense to release an updated version frequently (by April 2023, the book was on its 39th edition, which makes it nearly one revision a year). His recommendations were subject to change more often than most tourist activities. Prices change, shops go out of business, and areas of towns are updated. To accommodate that and help ensure that the books were reliable, Steves would update them regularly. This was relatively easy as he spent about 120 days in Europe every year. When the show was on the air, it was likely more than that, so he would have plenty of opportunity to verify the information in the books, even without the Internet (which was still a way from becoming common in the home during the early part of the 1990s).

Over most of the decade, he had a dedicated following because people wanted to know how to get around Europe on a tighter budget. It wasn't quite as efficient as online searches today, but quicker than reading a full book. In most cases, people would watch the shows, which tended to focus on one location and then supplement that advice from the book.

# CHAPTER 6

## *A Growing Audience*

TV was the best way to reach a wider audience during the latter part of the 20th century, but it was not the only way to attract more attention. With a successful show on the air and a set of books selling well, most people would probably feel they had more than enough on their plates. Not Steves, though. He used his new platform to enter a new media, which was incredibly popular during the 1990s – he started his own videotape series. He took his work for the show and extended it to provide more information and guidance that didn't make it to air because of time constraints.

Broadcasting on PBS aligned with his beliefs in making travel more accessible to a wider audience, just as he had indicated in his first book. The channel was free to everyone in the US, and the resources were readily available to anyone who wanted them. Expanding his appeal by offering videotapes was just another way to meet the needs of people who were interested but may have missed a particular show, a particular region hadn't been covered yet in the kind of detail he provided, or any other interruptions that life tends to throw at people. In addition, the videotapes allowed people to learn more and better plan. It was another way of supplementing their planning into a dream vacation. The first series was released in 1994, then another in 1995. Those who signed up to join Steves on one of his trips to Europe were given copies of the videotapes when they purchased their passes to travel. This helped to gain more attention to his business, and it became one of the most popular sources for people in the US to purchase Eurail passes.

Toward the end of the decade, PBS ended the show in 1998. It would only take about two years before Steve resumed his activity on TV, so it was a pretty short hiatus. However, the media landscape was already starting to change as the Internet had made it far easier for people to do their own research or look up information they needed. It wasn't nearly as robust as it is today, but people were starting to share details online. For younger people, they were able to connect with other young people online to get information. Still, many relied on more traditional methods of getting information, including Steves, who had a stellar reputation for providing the information needed to enjoy traveling across the western part of Europe.

He made the transition to helping people online with relative ease. However, even before the Internet played a critical role in shopping and planning, his show offered a newsletter that let people know more about what was happening within the company. It gained him a following worldwide, and those ardent supporters of his work are called "Rickniks." This likely helped bring his show back on air about two years after it had ended. The second version of his show had 11 seasons as of 2022.

With so many different types of media and ways of reaching audiences, the company went through a rebranding (something that was incredibly common as the Internet became instrumental for businesses to succeed). They determined that the best solution was to follow the same naming convention they had used for the videotapes, resulting in the new show being called *Rick Steves Europe*. His business was also renamed so that it was easier to locate the same information instead of people having to remember different names of his products based on how they typically accessed his media. The fact that he and his company figured this out so quickly speaks to how adept he is at business. Many large companies are gone today because they failed to adapt to the new online world. It was far more common for smaller businesses to fail because they tend to have different consistency in branding and messaging. His company adapted to working online, even if it was to a lesser extent in the early days. It flourished at a time when the travel industry faced a much greater crisis. Positions like travel agents are gone today because people do all of their work online, and there are so many resources that people can use themselves without paying a middleman. Part of what made it possible for Steves' company to thrive was that it was never like the more traditional businesses in the industry. The focus was on people getting a unique experience and trying things that interested a person. Steves didn't offer a "one-size-fits-all" approach to traveling. Instead, he gave people the tools and information they needed to go out and create their own experiences. This meant that their services became more in demand – it's exactly what people find online today when planning their own trips. What he offered was several decades ahead of its time. It was so universal that even before the Internet and the current method of exchanging information, it resonated with the people who watched or read his advice. This appeal continued today because he remains a reliable source of information on how to travel. If you talk to many people who have traveled to Europe, there is a good chance they consulted one of his many sources to get tips and tricks. Many of his business empire's roots today are rooted in the 1990s as things shifted and changed worldwide.

Today, he has a successful online presence, a wide

range of popular travel books, TV shows, newspaper columns, a radio talk show on NPR, and several other types of media that ensure people can get the information they need through the tools that are easiest for them. They even have an app that helps people while they travel.

# CHAPTER 7

## *Becoming an Advocate*

Steves unique approach to travel and business includes a heavy emphasis on working as an advocate. As someone who has lived all of his life along the west coast, it likely comes as no surprise that he identifies with the Democratic Party. However, there have been many times when he has been critical of the party. Considering how diverse the priorities of both parties are, hardly representing any single group of people in a nation of millions, it is more meaningful to say that he agrees with many of the stances that are important to people who live in the Pacific Northwest, particular west of the Cascade Mountain Range. Two of the causes for which he has been the biggest advocate are the legalization of cannabis and reforms to combat Climate Change.

As a resident of Washington State, he lives in one

of the first two states to have legalized the drug (both Colorado and Washington state legalized the use of marijuana on the same election night in 2012, making it legal for recreational use similar to alcohol and tobacco). His belief that cannabis should be treated like the other two popular US drugs began in the 1970s when he took a trip to Afghanistan. This was when he first tried one of the more traditional versions of the drug and said he enjoyed it.

The US has a long and complicated history with marijuana. Over most of the nation's history, its use was not treated like a crime. Not long after Prohibition failed in the US, Congress attempted to control the use of the plant, making the use of cannabis a crime in 1937. However, it wasn't until the 1970s that the US started to crack down on drug use. Initially, the US Congress had repealed most penalties associated with the drug, and they tried to establish regulations around it in 1972. However, President Richard Nixon rejected the recommendations made by Congress. In response to his rejection, 11 states established their own decriminalization laws.

In contrast, a majority of states significantly reduced penalties associated with it. Then in 1976, people who had been largely allowed to use drugs most of their lives decided they did not want their children using them. There was a movement by parents across the US to make stricter regulations.

President Regan sided with this stance, and the War on Drugs undid the laws and work done by the states to treat marijuana more as a soft drug. As soon as the federal government started to crack down, states started pushing back. Many of them had laws on the books governing the drug that was based on research indicating that cannabis is less addictive than the two legal drugs that are regulated by the US (alcohol and tobacco).

The US is hardly the only nation that treats marijuana like a hard drug while allowing the two more dangerous and addicting drugs to be used. As he has traveled Europe, Steves has seen how other nations have similarly cracked down on the drug in a way that they simply don't for alcohol and tobacco. Despite this, most people across North America and Europe continue to use it, making the national laws in strict opposition to what most people want. In the US alone, there is more support for the legalization of cannabis, with younger generations becoming increasingly more outspoken that it should not be criminalized. Washington and Colorado were just the first of 22 states that legalized it. At the same time, another nine have decriminalized the drug being used across the US. Washington, DC, Guam, the US Virgin Islands, and the Northern Mariana Islands have legalized cannabis. This is more of a push to restore decisions about the drug to the states instead of leaving it up to Presidents (who largely ignored the recommendations and desires expressed by Congress). Places like Washington and Colorado have shown how regulating it like alcohol and tobacco has also been a financial benefit. Many people across the country use cannabis regardless of the laws against it, similar to how Prohibition did not stop the consumption of alcohol.

Steves falls firmly on the side of people who want the drug to be treated like alcohol and tobacco, which starts with removing federal restrictions around marijuana. He has repeatedly expressed his advocacy of the drug over the years, once saying, "As a matter of principle, I believe the responsible adult recreational use of marijuana is a civil liberty. I'm a hard-working, kid-raising, church-going, tax-paying citizen of the United States, and if I work hard all day long and want to go home and smoke a joint and just stare at the fireplace for three hours, that's my civil liberty." This is a sentiment that is shared by a large percentage of Americans across the political spectrum. He has also framed the laws against cannabis in terms of civil rights and race "Marijuana is a drug, it can be abused, and it should be regulated, but the federal prohibition against marijuana is a disaster – it is racist, it is stoking a thriving black market, and it is counter-productive." Today, he continues to actively work toward removing federal regulations. He hosted a video program called *Marijuana: It's Time for a Conversation*, which earned a nomination from the Emmy Board.

His other major activism supports stricter regulation of activities contributing to Climate Change. As someone who lives in the Pacific Northwest, this focus should not come as much of a surprise as this is a part of the country that has been passing laws and regulations for several decades in an effort to counter the effects of carbon emissions and other contributors to the changing climate. His website has an entire page dedicated to what his company does to be more responsible toward treating the environment with greater care. Since traveling is often pointed to as a significant contributor to climate change, he has established his own carbon tax for the company that works to offset the contributions to the problem. As the website says, "Staying home isn't the answer. It's possible to mitigate this environment toll by supporting climate-smart initiatives in developing countries, where the need – and the potential for change – is greatest." This hints at the continued push for companies and large corporations to do more, as they are the primary contributor to the problem. Unfortunately, there is only so much that individuals can do. While they should still work to mitigate environmental damage, changes must be made by the largest contributors. That's why his business actively funds projects and groups that work to combat Climate Change.

# CHAPTER 8

## *Supporter of the Arts*

Having been raised in a family that values the arts and someone who has been able to travel Europe to see some of the works that are talked about hundreds to thousands of years after they were created, it should not be a surprise that Steves is a fervent supporter of the arts. More recently, his works and presentations have included a much greater emphasis on the arts. In an effort to help people better understand what there is to see, his company released Rick Steves Art of Europe. It was related as a part of the public television work that he has contributed to for decades but focuses on the different eras of European art, starting with the Stone Age. It provides six hours of things that would-be-European visitors may want to experience while they are in Europe, from famous works like David and the Sistine Chapel to cave paintings and relics of ancient times. There are more restrictions around viewing the older works, but there are still ways of viewing some of the earliest artwork of early Europeans.

Given his family history, it is perhaps a little surprising that Steves was a bit slower to warm up to the artistic aspects of Europe. While talking about the new series, he admitted, "I haven't always loved art history. As a teenager, I struggled doggedly through Kenneth Clark's epic art series... And I remember, back in my college days, flipping through a course catalog with dorm friends and playing 'name the most boring class of all.' My vote: Art History." A few professors and a life of travel have helped to better educate him on the value and interest in art. Since art has always reflected the world around it, many of the most well-known periods in European history are best depicted in their many art forms. It is one of the few ways to connect with people from thousands of years ago.

Given the number of wars across Europe over the millennia, architecture is more challenging to study. There has been a push to preserve and restore many different landmarks. However, far more have been lost to time and wars. For example, Hadrian's Wall remains from when the Romans invaded what is currently England. The wall was necessary because the Romans never fully conquered the island, and the Celtic people to the north (modern-day Scotland) could consistently repel attacks. The wall was meant to protect the Romans on the other side, and once it was a long structure that was impressive considering when it was made. Today there is very little left of it, largely because nature has reclaimed most of it. World Wars I and II destroyed countless architectural wonders. Since the rebuilding process post-World War II, there has been a real push to protect those left. Steves has recognized just how different being in front of or in some of these structures can shift how a person views their place in the world. As he once explained, "Climbing the dark spiral staircase in Paris' Saint-Chapelle and suddenly emerging in the most beautifully lit medieval chapel in Europe...a virtual lantern of 800-year-old stained glass built to house the crown of thorns. Turning our lights up in the monastery dining hall and seeing Leonardo's *Last Supper* come colorfully to life for our camera – and then realizing what a blessing it was for the friars, who for centuries ate in the silence under that fresco, to dine in such divine company." There are so many structures in Europe that can still inspire the mind and remind travelers of just how difficult life was compared to today and how much simpler it was. This makes traveling much more rewarding; people find a way to connect with history.

# CHAPTER 9

*Philanthropic Work*

Steves has traveled for decades focusing on seeing and experiencing things that are not the usual traveling experience. During his time, he has witnessed poverty and tragedy. Over the years, he has become a lesser-known philanthropist who continues to help where and when he can without the heralding that most philanthropists require. Instead, he focuses on helping those in need rather than being known for helping them.

His earliest philanthropic endeavors began during the 1990s while he gained attention on TV. Like many people who started to gain fame, his initial reaction was to give back to his community. Purchasing lands in and around Seattle, he worked to provide a place for homeless mothers, giving them a place where they could better take care of their children. Initially, he had planned to allow the building to help this particular demographic until he was ready to retire. At that time, he would sell the buildings to retire. That did not remain the plan, though, as he would continue to contribute, eventually giving away one apartment complex to the YWCA. Steves had no idea how far his business would go when he made the initial plan and by 2017, when he donated the complex. His business was far more profitable than he had ever thought possible. If he ever does retire (something that seems unlikely as he remains very involved in the business), he won't need to sell any of the buildings he purchased in the 1990s. This is despite the fact that those buildings are worth much more today than when he purchased them. As he said about the properties, "The mothers needed it more than I did."

One of his books, *Travel as a Political Act*, has become his way of helping to continue to fund the upkeep and maintenance of the buildings. The royalties from the book are donated to ensure they can continue providing a safer environment for children.

Much of his work to fight Climate Change is also part of his philanthropic endeavors. Traveling around the world, he has seen how different parts of the world have been affected and has wanted to offset the damage his business makes. The carbon tax he has imposed on his business brings in roughly a million dollars annually. All the money is invested in technologies and programs that make his tours carbon-neutral.

There have been several major disruptions to travel since the turn of the century as well. The first major event was 9/11, disrupting travel all over the world as people came to terms with the idea that people could use planes as weapons against civilians. Understanding how difficult travel would be in the post-9/11 world, Steves and his company strove to make people feel as safe as possible. It was a rough time for the company because traveling was difficult, and he had only recently restarted his TV show. Still, there was no reason to push people out of their comfort zone while coping with the shifts in the world following the terrorist attacks. Roughly a year after the event, people were ready and eager to travel again. Steves strove to ensure customers knew how to travel with all the new rules and regulations. The next major disruptor happened just as business was booming. Despite political unrest and civil issues, 2020 had been set to be one of the biggest years for traveling. Terrorism and other issues were far less of a concern, so people were eager to see new places. Then COVID-19 forced people to be locked into their homes during 2020. Many businesses were laying staff off and working to cut back. Despite being incredibly affected by the pandemic – travel was virtually impossible –Steves managed to keep the people in his company employed. They may not have been able to plan for trips, but they had all the necessary skills to help coordinate relief efforts in the community. They volunteered to meet social needs that needed to be addressed during the lockdown when services were overwhelmed. When most lockdowns were over, he resumed European tours in 2022. The notable exception was in Russia. When Russia invaded Ukraine in February 2022, he said that he wouldn't contribute any money to the Russian war by bringing in tourism money to the company.

# CONCLUSION

Though not necessarily well-known, Rick Steves is a staple in the travel community. He had decades of experience helping others see that traveling doesn't have to be a bank-busting endeavor. With the right approach, it's incredibly easy to make the plane tickets to your destination the most expensive part of the trip. Long before the Internet and the idea of life hacks, he provided just that to people interested in traveling. He offered advice that enabled college students to experience Europe despite their financial restrictions. His passion for travel became his career, even if that was not his original intention. He went from teaching a class to college students to managing several European tours a year. Responsible for numerous books on travel, he has become a go-to person for travel. Anyone who plans a trip abroad will almost certainly have read one of his books, watched his shows, or consulted his countless articles about advice for traveling. The man has created a unique place in a difficult industry because he has always focused on the experience, then tailored his recommendations to what he wants people to experience while abroad. Having been someone traveling on a tight budget in the early days, he has mastered how to find deals and hacks that significantly reduce the cost in other countries. While many tourist-focused companies focus on providing a particular type of experience that marks their clients as tourists, Steves' approach is to help people to travel more like the locals.

How he runs his business has proven beneficial to those who work for him and the community around the business. He managed to keep his staff employed during a pandemic, turning it into an opportunity to help the community. That was after decades of already supporting some of the most vulnerable people in the community for decades. Even during times of uncertainty, the ideas and philosophies have helped the man and his business to find their footing. He has always been very open about what he believes and why he believes it, which is baked into how he runs his travel business. This draws people to his work – a clear passion that benefits anyone willing to listen. And suppose it means a fantastic, unique trip to Europe. In that case, people will continue to listen to his advice for as many more years as he's willing to offer it.

Made in the USA
Middletown, DE
19 December 2023

46449002R00031